Boh Ramo Bokar

Mastering Folklore and Language Skills

Dr.*Nasi koje*

Aim and objective of the book:

1. To preserve and promote the culture of the Boh Ramo Bokar Communitiy of Shi Yomi District through learning second language (English).

2. To bring culture into the classroom and rooting the Boh Ramo Bokar children with their ancestors.

3. It brings culture into the ESL classroom as an educational function.

4. It educates the Boh Ramo Bokar children about concern and responsibility towards the values of dialects and identity as a whole.

5. Language preserves culture, the latter influences the language.

6. It enhances the folklore and folkliterature of Boh Ramo Bokar Community.

Learning English Through Boh Ramo Bokar Folkliterature

Volume II

The development of English Language book, especially for **the Boh Ramo Bokar** children using their native folksongs and folktales collected and translated into English by the reseacher. The materials and activities are developed by the reseacher. This textbook consists of five units arranged in a suitable order. After every folksong and folktale there are English Language activities developed by the researcher for the Boh Ramo Bokar children.

There is total eighteen activities. The activities are: **New Words, Reading is Fun, Let's Talk, Let's Act, Let's Share, Let's Draw, Let's Do, Let's Write, Say Aloud, Let's Listen, Let's Listen and Sing, Let's Sing, Let's Sing and Play, Let's Sing and Act, Let's Colour, Let's Find, Word Building, and Let's Practice**.

Like in book-I these activities are also arranged in a specific manner such that children will develop basic English Language Skills from each unit. It basically begins with "New Words" followed by "Let's Read", "Reading is Fun" and other activities. Like in book-1, each activity has specific motive such as "Let's Read" develops the reading skill in the children, "Let's Talk" develops the speaking skills in the children and so on. At the end of each unit there is a Teacher's Page for their references. And the Teacher's Page reflects the overall objective of the book.

CONTENTS

Unit-1

Ladies and Gentlemen

Abotani and Frog

Unit-2

An Insect

Abotani, Mouse and Rat

Unit-3

The Creator

Transformation of Abotani's Dogs into Wild Cat

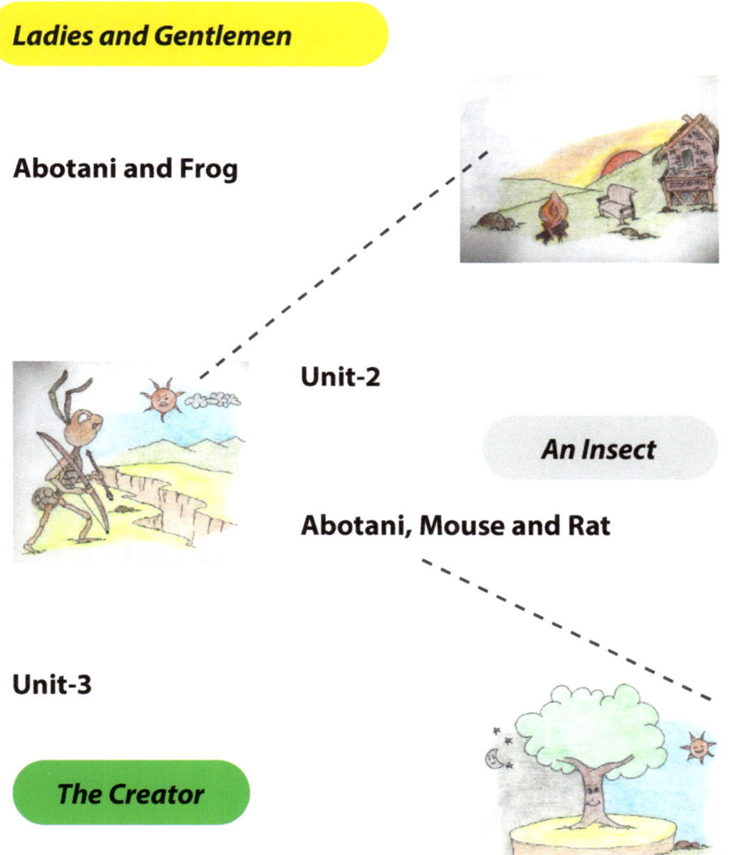

Unit-4

The Guide and the Maker

Abotani and Abing Chenah

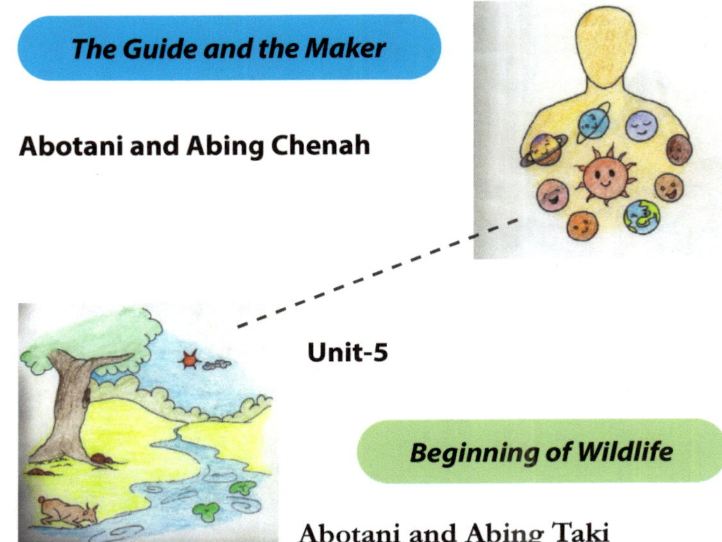

Unit-5

Beginning of Wildlife

Abotani and Abing Taki

Ladies and Gentlemen

Ladies and Gentlemen Jajinja,

It is a beautiful evening for the gathering Jajinja,

I welcome you all for this lovely evening, Jajinja

I am going to share you some story Jajinja,

In the olden days, there was no creatures Jajinja,

There were only nine suns and nine moons Jajinja,

Mother earth was dull and warm Jajinja,

Earth was not fit for survival Jajinja,

Billions of years an insect was born Jajinja,

Its name was Chingchup Diyup Jajinja,

Ladies and gentlemen Jajinja,

I hope you enjoyed the story Jajinja.

New words

beautiful   lovely   creature   dull   survival

Reading is fun

1. Who is "I" in this Folk Song?

2. How was the evening?

3. What was the story about?

4. Tell something about the mother Earth?

5. Who were gathering in a beautiful evening?

6. What is a name of insect in the poem?

Let's talk

1. Have you ever gathered around fire in winter with family?

2. What do you do when you gather around the fire?

3. Have you ever told a story before?

4. Have you ever heard of word "Jajinja" before?

5. Do you like to gather around the fire?

Let's act

Imagine it's a winter and act like you are sitting around the fire and tell a short story.

Let's listen

Grasshopper is an insect who like to jump.

Ant is an insect who likes to run.

Butterfly is an insect who likes to fly.

Fire fly is an insect who likes to light.

Let's write

Circle the words that can be used and needed to light a fire.

Match-Box	Paper	Knife
Table	Pen	Wood
Chair	Lighter	Bag

Make a sentence using the word you have circled above:

____

____

Let's practise

LADIES AND GENTLEMEN

LADIES AND GENTLEMEN

LADIES AND GENTLEMEN

LADIES AND GENTLEMEN

LADIES AND GENTLEMEN

LADIES AND GENTLEMEN

Abotani and Frog

Millions of years ago the mother earth gave birth plants, insects, animals, the human being Abotani and Ame Tahor. Abotani and Ame Tahor were supernatural creatures. Ame Tahor was the first female and Abotani was the first male being on the earth. Abotani had tried fatherhood with Many creatures on earth but did not bear any successor. Later he married a frog.

She was a dutiful wife but she always used to eat the left-over half burnt food which Abotani did not like. So due to anger Abotani pushed her. The Frog was shocked and jumped into the fire, and got burnt. Abotani got mad with the fire for burning his wife. He tried to attack the fire but failed. Abotani's marriage with the frog was not successful.

Moral: *The moral of the story is that one should learn to accept and comprise in marriage. It also educates to control one's anger and develop humbleness.*

New words

Supernatural   Creatures   Successor   Dutiful   Burnt.

Reading is fun

1. Whom did mother earth give birth to?

2. Who were the first female and male on earth?

3. Whom did Abotani get married to?

4. What kind of wife is Abotani's wife?

Let's talk

1. Have you heard of "Abo Tani" before?

2. Have you ever seen a frog?

3. Do you know what frog eat?

Say aloud

My mother is a dutiful wife.

She cooks very tasty food for us.

She loves us more than herself.

Let's colour

Colour the frog

Let's listen and sing

ABOTANI

Abotani Abotani where are you.

We your children always remember you.

Abotani Abotani make me strong like you.

So that I can live and grow old like you

Let's write

1. Find a suitable word from the story and choose the word from the box:

> dutiful mad supernatural fatherhood married

Abotani and Ame Tahor were _________ creatures.

Abotani had tried __________ with Many creatures on earth.

Later he ___________ a frog. She was a ___________wife.

Abotani got ________ with the fire for burning his wife.

2. Find suitable opposite words from story and Write in the space:

Father   ___________

Predecessor   ___________

Full   ___________

Pulled   ___________

Passed   ___________

3. Write five lines on My Mother:

____

____

____

Let's do 

Plant a sampling of any tree in your school and Take care of it until it grows strong.

Teacher's Pages Unit-1

As we begin this book let us recall a few ideas that were reflected in Book One:

- We need to keep in mind that there is also a transition from the home language to the school language when we teach English at this level. Apart from moving from the mother tongue to the second and third language, it is a move to the more disciplined environment of the school, where social behaviour is to be polished and related to a group of peers.

- Thus, learning English need not involve the loss of their home language.

- Attempts are made in the book to draw on what is familiar to the child because while the child is being exposed to new ideas and worlds, she is still rooted in present environments.

- The book supports the child by focusing mainly on emotional needs and anxieties in order to strengthen the pathways to learning process.

- Imaginative boost is given by the use of games and tasks that draw on the imagination, the child will see that organised play and work have their own rules and discipline.

- The book helps the child in development of a child as a social being by encouraging the child to use language in speech and writing, to express feelings and opinions, to reach out to others, to interact with others, see other points of view.

- Keeping in mind the age of children and their way of thinking, the activities in books are written in such a way that the child learns through fun and enjoyment, music, games and activity. Hence, there should be as much movement as possible, so that the child gets to use language without much conscious effort.

- Compliment and encourage the child for efforts and performance by using phrase like 'that's good' or 'let's try again' or 'do you want to change what you have done?' rather than using stricter forms of speech.

- Remember every child is special and have different abilities such as some are musically inclined/ physically active / mathematically inclined /more introvert? Find ways to motivate and encourage each one to participate actively in the class? Be gentle and sweet when you communicate with the class; try to explain in as simple as possible with examples also rephrase in different words if they do not understand words given in the folktale first for the first time. Keep in mind that each child has different speed of learning so let children work at their own speed.

In this Book main focus has been laid on all the language skills such as:

Listening and speaking

Read the folksong and folktale aloud, before you ask children to recite or repeat. This will give exposure to the sounds of language and help in development. Ask children to guess the meanings by using whatever knowledge of the word and of language they already have before giving meanings. For **Say aloud** activity, it is advised to practice the sounds of words yourself first, before you start repeating them in class.

Speaking on issues relevant to the child's life based on the theme of the folksong and folktale is to be done in **Talk time**. Motivate and encourage the child to talk in English during the process that way it will help him/her to increase the use of English. You are advised to keep the environment encouraging, free from stress and fear, and motivating during the talk time and other activities as well.

Reading

By now, the children must be capable of reading on his/her own so let them guess meanings of difficult words from the folksong and folktale by choosing options that are given in the book or which you can give. Let the child read on their own with understanding this will develop their reading skill. All the meanings might not be understood at once so let them realise them on their own.

Writing

Just like in book one, writing continues with special focus on the running hand. This is will develop their eye and hand coordination which is very important at this stage. It is a request to you that –

- Please note that the child does not lift the pencil from the book while practicing running hand till a word has been completed

- The child has the correct grip on the pencil.

- Without overloading the child at this stage with writing give extra practice for writing.

The various activities for writing like paper tearing, cutting pasting, colouring within boundaries, stringing beads using spoons for transferring rice from one bowl to another for instance are all important means for developing good handwriting at this stage.

Note: Encourage and let the children use whichever hand they are comfortable with for writing.

Just like in Book One, divide the class into groups for various activities also name the group by different names etc.

Dramatise emotions like being shy, happy, excited or angry children to improve their expressive skills and building confidence in oneself.

Unit 1 focus on the origin of the earth and its creatures making the child familiar with nature and its creatures because the tribal society is completely dependent on the nature and its gift. The unit gives the idea of Abotani the fore father of Tani clan and his life. It teaches to be compassionate and compromising. It also educates to control one's anger and develop humbleness.

An Insect

Chingchup Diyu Jajinja,

There was an insect named Chingchup Diyup Jajinja,

Chingchup had a son who was his everything Jajinja

But heat of the sun killed his son.

Chingchup Diyup morn for day and night Jajinja,

Chingchup Diyup determines to take revenge Jajinja,

So, he made bows and arrows with his power.

Sun always rise on the east Jajinja,

Before the sunrise, he shot into the eyes of sun Jajinja,

And there was darkness everywhere on the mother earth Jajinja,

Chingchup Diyup Jajinja.

New words

Insect   Morn   Determine   Rise   Darkness

Reading is fun

1.   Who is Chingchup diyu?

2.   How did Chingchup diyu son die?

3.   What does he do to the sun?

4.   From which side does the sun always rise?

Let's talk

1.   Have you ever walked in a sunny day?

2.   What is the shape of sun?

3.   Have you ever seen an insect?

4.   What do you call sun and moon in your local language?

5.   Name any five insects in English and their names in local language?

Let's draw

Make a group of five children each. Each group take a chart paper. Follow the steps.

1. Each group draw an insect.

2. The first child draws insect's head.

3. The second child draws his tentacles.

4. The third child draws the arms.

5. The fourth draws his legs.

6. The fifth child colours the insects.

7. Look at the insect. Isn't he a funny insect? Name him.

Let's practice:

Insect Insect Insect Insect
Jajinja Jajinja Jajinja Jajinja
Son   Son   Son   Son
Night Night   Night   Night
West   West   West   West

Abotani, Mouse and Rat

Once upon a time, Abotani's maize were stolen from the field by some unknown person. When he followed the foot print of the stranger, it led him to the house of a rat named Jajak Kojak. Abotani charged him. But the Rat refused the allegation. Rather he blamed a Mouse named Abing Pacheng. Abotani extended his thanks and reached the house of a Mouse. When Abotani condemned him, the mouse denied the criticism. The mouse turned extremely mad against the Rat and swiftly marched towards the house of Jajak Kojak.

The moment he arrived, he heard the rat singing a happy song, "I am Jajak Kojak, I have stolen maize of Abotani. I am using maize as mattress and pillow. I am very happy because I have abundant to eat." The mouse hearing the song turned angry, with a burning piece of wood hit on the chest of the rat, and ran back to his house. Jajak Kojak ran after him but could not enter his house due to his body. When he pushed his tail to kill the mouse, in return Abing Pacheng held his tail tightly and pulled out the skin of the tail. As a result of his cleverness and pride the rat has white spot on his chest and tail. The white spots on the body of rats show to avoid lies and pride.

Moral: *The story educates the Boh Ramo Bokar learners to have self-respect and to be humble. It also conveys us not to lie and be proud, it might cause harm in one's life and family. One should never underestimate a person by his looks and size because the appearance can be deceptive.*

New words

Stolen   Condemn   Allegation   Denied   Abundant

Reading is fun:

Put a (✓) or a (✗) against the following sentences. One has been done for you.

Abotani's maize were stolen from the field by Jajak Kojak. (✓)

a. Abing Pacheng was singing a happy song. (✓)

b. The mouse turned extremely mad against the Rat and swiftly marched towards the house of Jajak Kojak. ( )

c. When Abotani condemned him, the mouse denied the criticism. ( )

d. The white spots on the body of rats show to avoid lies and pride. ( )

e. Jajak Kojak hold Abing Pacheng's tail tightly and pulled out the skin of the tail. ( )

1. Who did steal the maize from Abotani's field?

2. Who is Jajak Kojak?

3. Who is Abing Pacheng?

4. Can Jajak Kojak Sing a song?

5. Who did Abotani Condemn?

Let's talk

1. Have you seen maize before?

2. Do you like to eat maize?

3. Can you sing a song?

4. Do you like to Sing?

Let's listen

The Maize that we grow.

Maize is yellow inside and green outside.

Maize is also called Corn. 

This comes from the Spanish word 'maiz'.

Corn is a cereal crop that belongs to the grass family.

The cob or ear of corn is actually part of the flower and an individual kernel is a seed.

An ear of corn has at least 800 kernels in 16 rows.

And I just love the corn that we grow in our paddy field.

Silence game- Quiet Statues

This simple game always brings a smile!

1. Start with Quietly whispering to the kids what kind of statue you want them to make.

2. Some ideas are a rat, a monkey, an elephant, a mommy, a daddy, a policeman, a bear, a tiger or even the Abotani statue.

Now at the count of three, the kids have to freeze into their statue and then you pick the best statue. After that, this person then whispers to the kids what kind of statue to make next, and so the game repeats.

And Remember, statues don't talk or move!

Let's share

What would you call these pictures in your local language?

SUN:_________________

BUTTER-FLY:_____________

STAR:____________

MOON:___________________________

Let's act

Act out the story. Play the parts of the Abotani, Jajak Kojak and Abing Pacheng in turns in the classroom.

Say aloud

Mouse House

Rat   Fat   Bat

Maize   Rice   Dice   Mice

Let's find

Find the words given below in the BOX:

MOUSE   RAT
MAIZE   MICE
SONG   FIELD

A	M	O	U	S	E	B
R	A	T	C	A	L	I
F	I	E	L	D	S	A
O	Z	M	I	C	E	U
T	E	E	T	Q	A	M
S	O	S	O	N	G	A

Word building

Look at the letters given below and make words starting with them.

L ______________   ______________   ______________

Q ______________   ______________   ______________

O ______________   ______________   ______________

S ______________   ______________   ______________

N ______________   ______________   ______________

Let's write:

Circle the odd one out

Rat	Fat	Sat	Get
House	Mouse	roused	Fuse
Way	Say	They	Pay

Fill in the blanks with a suitable word as in story:

Once upon, a time _______________ were stolen from the field. (Maize/Rice)

The mouse turned extremely ____________against the rat. (Mad/Bed)

Mouse heard the Rat _________________ a happy song. (dancing/singing)

The white spots on the body of rats show to avoid ___________ and _______. (lies or truth, pride or proud)

Who said these words in the story?

"I am jajak kojak, I have stolen maize of Abotani" _______________________.

"My maize was stolen from the field by some unknown person"_______________.

"I am very happy because I have abundant to eat" _______________________.

Look at the pictures, give the animal or birds name:

Dog	Hen	Sparrow	Duckling

____

________________   ________________

____

Teacher's Pages   Unit-2

Unit-2 is an opportunity to share with children the love and connection between the father and his son with special reference to the folksong *An Insect* (Chingchup Diyu). It shows how a father goes beyond the extend to fight for the pain he has experienced through death of his son. *Abotani, Mouse and Rat* (Abotani, Pacheng holoka Jajak Kojak) teaches the children the meaning of self-respect and to be humble in nature along with the importance of God's creation. Lies can never be an option for happiness because there will always be a consequence, so one should learn to be happy being what they are and what they have.

Share this verse with the class after the activity –

"Family means everything.

Family is always there to rely Upon.

Family is not always about the blood

But the ones that are there in the time of need

And willing to hold your hands

And stand by you in the good and bad times of your life.

So, always love your family."

The movements, actions, activities of different insects and rats/mouse can be discussed. Folktales can be shared in their own language.

Develop listening skills

This Unit involves the children in playing a game called silence game (Quiet Statues). Let them all be gently guided to instructions given in the game mentioned and enjoy the game. This will develop mindfulness in children through an ability to gain awareness of the noise surrounding them and exercise self-control in them.

The motive of this game is to develop in children a habit for listening. Also introduce various other such activities that develop their listening skills like practicing rhymes with actions. Also introduce meditation which is a very useful breathing exercise.

Develop vocabulary

The vocabulary games will improve vocabulary along with encouraging and letting the children enjoy as they learn new words. The teachers can start by writing four capital letters on the board. Each student chooses one and note it down. Now start with writing lower case letters on the board like previous one. Again, let each child choose one and note it. Continue on writing 3-4 letters at a time and let students complete the words. With the completion of each new words, you may start with a new word (using a capital letter).

Exposure to language

- Give names of wild animals, domestic animals, insects and birds to each child and let children build words related to what they know and like or hate about it. e.g., when having a game where they can describe those mentioned creatures, like: The Spider is brown in colour and it is really good at making nets. Keep adding names of such animals, insects and birds. Let them have a class activity for the same.

Serial No.	Name	Share something about it
1	Spider	
2	Lion	
3		

Develop writing skills

Unit 1 and 2 mainly focuses on the revision of the writing skills of Book One. At this stage the children are encouraged to listen words pronounced by the teacher (such as in apple) and create the pictures of it (that is followed by sentence formation).

Develop the ability to follow directions

TOP   MIDDLE   BOTTOM

Construct a bamboo cupboard box and involve the class in the construction and then paint the top shelf- blue, the middle – Yellow and the bottom shelf – Red. After the completion of cupboard construction place different items available in the class room at all the shelfs. Now, have the children identify and describe what they see in the top, middle and bottom shelf of the cupboard.

The Creator

The mighty Meku-Meteh Jajinja,

Meku-Meteh the creator Jajinja,

Meku-Meteh for understanding
the darkness on earth Jajinja,

Meku-Meteh for creating Sun and Moon Jajinja,

And there was brightness again Jajinja.

The powerful Meku-Meteh Jajinja,

For making earth warmer Jajinja,

For the ray of hope Jajinja,

The first species kingdom of plants Jajinja,

Meku-Meteh Jajinja.

New words

Creator Brightness Powerful Hope Species Kingdom

Let's read

There is light during day because of sun.

There is light in the night because of moon.

Reading is fun

1. What is the meaning of Meku-Meteh?

2. Can you write two things created by Meku-Meteh?

3. Who removed the darkness from earth?

Let's Listen

1. Have you ever wondered who created this beautiful earth?

2. What is difference between sun and moon?

3. Have you ever watched a night sky during full moon?

Say aloud

SUN	NAAN	DONE	BEGUN
RAYS	MAZE	HAZE	BAYS
MOON	SOON	NOON	SPOON

Riddle time

I am Double in the moon and none in sun. who am I?

Let's write

Play the game with your friends. Gather around a table with your friends and place a pencil on the table and spin it. Close your eyes. The person towards whom the sharpen part of the pencil faces has to write the names of five things asked by the friends.

____

____

____

____

____

Let's practise

Sun   Sun   Sun   Sun

Moon   Moon   Moon   Moon

Earth Earth   Earth Earth

Ray   Ray   Ray   Ray   Hope   Hope   Hope   Hope

Transformation of Abotani's Dogs into Wild Cat

One day Abotani's bajra field was eaten up by an unknown creature. So, he decided to hunt the creature with the help of his hunting dogs Tarongongbo and Pungchirinyi. They

run after the animals but could not catch. Abotani got tired. While taking rest he plucked a colour wood and pink colour leaves. He kept them inside his bag. The strange animal ran so fast crossing different layers of mountains. The animal entered inside a house made up of rocks followed by Abotani and his dogs.

There was two Tibetian ladies inside the house; the animal was their pet horse. They could not understand each other's language. So, they communicated through gestures. Abotani gave the ladies colour wood and pink leaves. These ladies in return gave two pieces of rock salt and advised him to use for cooking.

Abotani kept the salt inside the bag, and returned home along with his hunting dogs. He marked the tree trunks and stones, so that he could identify them in the future trips. But due to long journey and shortage of food, his dogs could not move anymore. So, through his preaching he converted them into wild cat, and left them in the forest. Traditionally wild cats are called as Sayin and Sarki. Till today the hunter find these animals in the jungle.

Moral: *The moral of the story is that one should take risk to take up any journey because it might lead you to a beautiful destination. For example, in the above tale Abotani's energy to chase the unknown animals took him to the discovery of salt for humanity today. The tale also educates us about the glance of Ramo wild animals, and the use of salt*

New words

Hunt   Plucked   Communicated   Gesture   Trunk

Reading is fun

1. Who decided to hunt the creature with the help of hunting dog?

2. How many ladies were there in house?

3. How did Abotani and Tibetian Ladies Communicate?

4. What were given to Abotani by the Tibetian ladies?

5. What animals did the dogs turned into by Abotani?

Let's talk

1. Have you ever gone to a jungle? How does it feel?

2. What kind of sound does the dog make?

3. Do you have a dog in your home or in surrounding? Tell something about it?

4. Tell the difference between salt and sugar?

Say aloud

Creature	Nature	Gesture
Dog	Log	Jog
Pink	Ink	Sink

Let's write

Fill in the blanks using the suitable word from the box by reading folktale.

communicated   hunt   fast   gestures   catch

1. He decided to _________ the creature with the help of his hunting dogs

2. They run after the animals but could not___________.

3. The strange animal ran so ____________crossing different layers of mountains.

4. They _________________through____________.

Put the letters in order to make a word. One has been done for you.

etena   <u>Eaten</u>

uhnt   ______

pikn   ______

bga   ______

owod   ______

crok   ______

meho   ______

rete   ______

tac   ______

Look at the pictures and choose the words given below:

Treetrunk   Dog   House   Mountain   House
Rock   bird

___

___

___

Teacher's Pages   Unit-3

This Unit highlights the idea of creator along with the birth of wild Cat. The emphasize is on widening social horizons of children and it is a good opportunity to introduce the importance of taking risk in life and being grateful to others, where children learn to share, help and develop a gratitude towards things around  them. They must also be introduced with the concept of discipline and its importance in their life. Encourage them to be discipline and follow the rules and not to be aggressive on the playground. Discuss the meaning of risk and taking risk in one's life.

Develop listening skills

Read the folksong and the folktale aloud with suitable expression and hand actions. Let the class guess and tell the meaning of difficult words. You are requested to avoid explanation as much as possible, especially of folktales. Let them arrive at their own conclusion, which they can change or improvise by listening to class discussions and to other children.

- This will help you in observing the children whether they are listening or just pretending to be listening. If you feel that they are fumbling, you can backtrack and involve them in reading the folksong and the folktale aloud.

- No need to explain the meanings immediately, let them guess instead.

Group Time

Discuss with the class how salt is made, science behind it and Only iodine rich salt is needed to be used for consumption. Talk about how it would feel if there is no salt in the food and what would happen to their health if the salt is not included in their regular diet.

Develop vocabulary

- To develop the vocabulary in children let the children enact the folktale with expression and actions under your assistance and instruction. Let the children make a face mask of persons and animals and other creatures such Abotani, Dogs, Tibetian Ladies, cats, salt, plants on the chart paper and cut it out. Before cutting out of masks from chart paper let them colour it with suitable colors. Bring the traditional attires for the Abotani and Tibetian Ladies. Make sure that everybody participates by making sounds like the creatures in the jungle and actions of the creatures.

- Play word games with the children to help improve children's spelling, reading, and vocabulary. You are Requested to include word games such as "Hang Man", "I spy", "Bingo", "Word Family Game", "Word Search", "Unscramble the words", "Categories", "Words within a word", "I am going on a picnic", and "Story prompts". This word games encourage conversation and early literacy that you can play on the spot or prepare yourself with just some blackboard, paper and pencil. Help and join the children in the word games. Also explain 'doing' words (these could be enacted as well), opposites, rhyming words etc. with more examples of your own along with encouraging the children to give their own examples. Keep in mind that the participation of all children is more important than their giving correct answers, for interest will surely increase the will to learn.

- Use contextual words like 'risk', 'fast', 'strong', 'weak', 'happy'

Exposure to language

Let children build sentence with – dog   log   jog

Lead and encourage them to weave sentences using these words like –

- Do you have dog?
- Have you seen log?

Develop speaking skills

Sounds of words using: O — Oates, Odd, Onion, On, Obese.

F — Fan, Forest, Funny, Fat.

N.B.: *When we say 'F' we bite our lips. When we say 'O' the lips go round and do not meet.*
Conversation based on 'Role-play'.

- Divide your class in four groups and let them play with letters.

Develop writing skills

Look over the student's grip on the pencil (especially the tripod grip) and help individual children write words using letters from A to Z but remember let the children use whichever hand they are convenient with whether it may be left or right and encourage them.

You can write the alphabet and words on chart paper and hang them in the class.

You make it interesting by making the child write her/his name under the alphabet with which her/his name starts and also by making the use of letters in his/her name. In case of letters with which no name starts involve children in a class activity of coining new words to write under those letters.

The Guide and the Mak

Runeh is the guide Jajinja,

Penah is the creator Jajinja,

Runeh-Penah is invisible Jajinja,

Runeh-Penah is unseen Jajinja,

Runeh-Penah is unheard Jajinja,

Runeh-Penah is unfelt Jajinja,

Runeh-Penah is strong Jajinja,

Runeh-Penah is re-creator Jajinja,

Runeh-Penah is everywhere Jajinja,

New words

Guide   Invisible   Unfelt   Strong   Re-creator

Reading is fun

1. Who is Runeh?

2. Who is Penah?

Let's talk

1. Do you know earth was created billions of years ago?

2. Have you ever heard of planets before?

3. Can you name the planets of our solar system?

4. Do you know sun is at the centre of the solar system earth rotates around it?

Let's Listen

GUIDE WIDE   RIDE

UNSEEN   GREEN BEEN

STRONG   WRONG   LONG

Let's Share

1. What do you call "Creator" in your language?

2. Have you ever guided someone in anything?

Let's sing

Dear Creator! Dear Creator!

Thank for This Beautiful World

Thank You for the Happiness and Love in our life

I will keep this world beautiful and Happy

Creator! Creator!

Take away All our Sadness and Difficulties.

Let's write

Choose the correct word and Fill in the blanks with the words given below in the box:

1. Runeh-Penah is __________Jajinja, (invisible/ visible)

2. Runeh-Penah is __________Jajinja, (unheard/ heard)

3. Runeh-Penah is __________ Jajinja, (felt/ unfelt)

4. Runeh-Penah is __________ (weak/strong)

Abotani and Abing Chenah

Long ago there was a dangerous devil called Abing Chenah on this earth. He was the enemy of Abotani. He used to disturb in every progressive activity of Abotani. Those days Abotani was cultivating two types of crops named 'Yahi' and 'Lakka'. But Chenah by his magical power destroyed Abotani's crops by inserting some cane bushes in Yahi. Till today the brush type of hair is still seen inside of Yahi plant.

With the power of his eyes, he converted Lakka as bitter plant and till today it tastes bitter. Since then Abotani stop the cultivation of Yahi and Lakka plants in the field. It was left in the forest and still grows in the forest.

At the same time Abotani was very angry by the frequent destruction cause by Chenah, it was very difficult to make any kind of progress.

He thought of ideas day and night to escape from him. So, one fine day a great idea of making friendship with Nyulung Yapung (the Goddess of wind) and Jiney Taying (the Goddess of swift transformation) strike to Abotani. Then he invited Chenah for a lunch in a lonely place. Abotani prepared rice and fish. He cooked some slice of fish inside two big bamboos on fire. Before Chenah could use his power and see the poisoned fish, Abotani called the Goddess of wind and storm. She appeared with sound, dust and particles covered Chenah's eyes.

Again, Abotani called the Goddess of quick transformation and replaced the bamboo of roasted fish with poisoned. The moment they had the lunch Chenah's body turn black and pale. He requested Abotani to covey his last message to the animals, creatures, land and water of earth to visit him. Abotani thought he is dying and accepted his last wish. He quickly moved around the earth and spread the news of Chenah's death. From that very day, those creatures who visited him before the death turned into poisonous animals. These are water, bees, snakes, centipede, scorpion, spiders, frogs, fish, mosquitoes, fire ants etc.

Moral: *The moral of the tale is that one should never underestimate the ability of a person. He or she can do anything when situation compels. It also educates that frequent torturing and harming other can give birth to a poisonous plot and destructive enemy.*

New words

Strike   Dangerous   Progressive   Bitter   Frequent Transformation   Poisonous

Reading is fun

1. What type of crop were cultivated by Abotani?

2. Who was the enemy of Abotani?

3. What is the name of Goddess of wind and swift transformation?

Let's talk

1. Have you ever gone to a paddy field and how does it feel?

2. Have you ever seen people cooking food in bamboo?

3. Can you name your national animal and bird?

4. Name your state animal and bird?

5. What would you call those above-mentioned animals and birds in your local language?

Team Time

Do you know what kind of cultivation is most preferred in hilly region? why?

And what kind of crops are grown. Sit in a group and discuss about it.

Let's write

Write five lines about your best friend.

____

____

____

____

____

Let's Sing and Play

Ring-a-ring o' roses,

A pocket full of posies,

A-tishoo! A-tishoo!

We all fall down.

- W. W. Newell

Let's practise

POWER   POWER   POWER   POW-
ER

BITTER   BITTER   BITTER   BITTER

GREAT   GREAT   GREAT   GREAT

KIND   KIND   KIND   KIND

IDEAS   IDEAS   IDEAS   IDEAS

Teacher's Pages   Unit-4

The main motive in **Unit 4**, is to further assist and encourage children to build their imagination by listening carefully, reading, speaking and writing sentences.

Developing listening skills

If the breathing exercises have been introduced as suggested in Unit 2, the children would gradually have learnt to stay calm and if not then introduce in this unit. As the breathing exercise in unit 2 let them sit with their eyes closed as if in a thinking pose. Now read the folksong slowly and in audible voice for two or three times so that they can take in the beauty of folksong and also be a part of it. Only after the completion of reading ask them to open their eyes and read the folksong with proper and audible voice. After that encourage them to recite it with suitable gestures and actions.

For listening skills

In order to improve the listening skills of children you can use recorded sounds of items and objects such as stones, pebbles, water, dust, salt, sugar, bell etc. by putting them inside a container/ box that are available in the vicinity.

Before playing the sound ask the students to close their eyes. Then make the sound and ask them to identify the sound by categorizing it into sound like soft, hard, low, loud. Teach the children how to use dictionary and encourage the children them to learn the pronunciation and word meanings from it.

Let the children read the folktale after you are done reading and discussing the folktale as the teacher reads, pupils become familiar first with the folktale in spoken language and the illustration, gradually an acquaintance develops with the print code. So, the more confident she/he feels in reading, the more motivated she/he will be. Also note down the words in chart that you want the children to learn. Ask children if they have seen the night sky and what they saw and the colours they see in them. And lastly ask them to make sentences.

Develop speaking skills

Try to build up the vocabulary of the children on the different crops grown in winter and summer. Other than that, discuss about the various food source from the jungle.

Discuss about the importance of bamboo in a tribal society with them. Ask them in what ways bamboos are being used in their locality. Talk about use of bamboo and bamboo crafts in the local rituals.

In the folksong **Runeh-Penah (The Guide and the Maker)** planets around the chest is used. This word 'planets' says more about creator (the naming word), involve children in describing the planets and other celestial objects they can see in the night sky, e.g. moon, sun, stars, planets, etc.

Introduce children to the following set of rules
1. Take turns
2. Listen quietly
3. Speak clearly

Group activity

Divide the class into different groups and name the groups. Each group is to be asked to discuss what they like about fishing and what they don't, giving reasons for the same.

Develop writing skills

Make children write meaningful and constructive sentences. (My best friend, My family, My aim in life...). And while writing let their best friend sit beside them so that they can describe each other well.

Ready to follow instructions

Introduce children to "talking on the cellphone" using polite words for conversation. Bamboo can be used to make mock phones in the class. Help them in making the cell phone. Let two volunteers be there from the children and take turns to speak on the phone to each other using polite words.

Beginning of Wildlife

Our ancestor narrates the beginning of wildlife Jajinja,

The say change of climate gave birth to new life Jajinja,

They say change of climate gave birth to kingdom of plants Jajinja,

They say change of climate gave birth to kingdom of animals Jajinja,

They say change of climate gave birth to earthly life Jajinja,

They say change of climate gave birth to human life Jajinja,

They say universe started with beauty of wildlife Jajinja,

Our ancestor narrates the beginning of wildlife Jajinja.

New words

Ancestor   Wildlife   Gave   Climate   Beauty

Reading is fun

1. What does changes of climate gave birth to?

2. How does universe start?

Let's talk

1. Do you know the difference between Climate and weather?

2. What Climate do you like the most?

Let's listen

Put a () or a (✗) against the following sentences. One has been done for you.

1. They say change of climate gave birth to new life Jajinja.
   (✓)

2. They say change of climate did not gave birth to kingdom of animals Jajinja ( )

3. They say change of climate gave birth to human life Jajinja. ( )

3. They say change of climate gave birth to kingdom of plants Jajinja, ( )

4. They say change of climate gave birth to kingdom of insects Jajinja, ( )

5. They say universe started without beauty of wildlife Jajinja. ( )

Say aloud

Ancestor Creator Director

Climate Mate Estimate Private

Birth Earth Dearth Berth Ward

Kingdom Freedom Wisdom Random Seldom Boredom

Let's sing and act

Dear Plant Dear Plant

Thank You for The Food

Thank You for the fresh Air

That we breathe in.

Let's write

Complete the words using a, e, i, o, and u.

1. _nc_st_r

2. K_ngd_m

3. Cl_m_t_

4. _n_v_rs_

5. B_ _ _ty

Let's do

Using your imagination draw a beautiful Scenery.

Let's practise

Change of Climate
Change of Climate
Change of Climate
Change of Climate
Change of Climate

Abotani and Abing Taki

Once upon a time there were two bothers Abotani and Abing Taki. They were born from the same womb of mother earth. Both brothers became well known hunters. They used to hunt animals together with their weapons. After many years Abing Taki started consuming raw flesh of animals in the forest itself. He stopped bringing meat of animals at home. One day Abotani asked him, "why are you not eating cooked meat? Why have you stopped bringing your hunted animals at home?" Abing Taki replied, "I appreciate raw meat more than cooked meat." Forest is more suitable place for him to live. When Abotani heard these words he became very sad, because they were going to be separated.

Abing Taki requested Abotani to cover his body with grasses and bushes in the forest. After three days remove the covered grass and bushes from his body. Abotani fulfilled his request and went back to home. After three days Abotani visited the same place and removed the covered grass and bushes. Abotani was shocked and scared of Abing Taki because he had totally transformed into a tiger. He had hair on his body and head of a Tiger. Abing Taki requested Abotani not to tell anybody about his transformation into a Tiger. "If you tell anyone about this incident, I will kill you." Abotani promised "I will never tell anyone till my death". In this way, Abotani and Abing Taki promised each other to keep the incident as secret.

After thousands of years later when Abotani became very old, he was sitting close to the fire and doing cane works with knife. He told the secret behind his separation with his elder Abing Taki to his son. The story was never ending and during the narration, Abotani's knife fell under the house through the wide gaps of bamboo floor of his house. Abotani told his son to get his knife but the son could not find his knife. At last, Abotani came outside of his house searching his fallen knife. Abing Taki attacked him at the neck and killed him as he had broken the promise made before.

Moral: *This tale educates Boh Ramo Bokar children about the importance of promise. It also shows the human and non-human creature. Boh Ramo community strongly believed in supernatural powers. When the community members make promise, they used the Tiger jaw as an agent of the supernatural power to swear, accompanied by chants of the priest. Boh Ramo Bokar believed that like in the folktale the Tiger will kill him or her if they break the promise.*

New words

Womb Consuming Appreciate Fulfilled Incident Narration

Reading is fun

1. Once upon a time there were two ____________ Abotani and Abing Taki. (Sisters/Brothers)

2. Abing Taki requested Abotani to cover his body with ______________ and ______________ in the forest. (grasses and bushes/ woods and clothes)

3. Who said these words in the story?

"why are you not eating cooked meat? Why have you stopped bringing your hunted animals at home?".

"If you tell anyone about this incident, I will kill you."

____

4.What are Abotani and Abing Taki well-known for?

5.What did Abing Taki transform into and why?

6.Why did Abing Taki Killed Abotani?

Let's listen

Father   Mother, Together   Gather, Grass   Brass, Tell   Well, Knife   Wife, Old   Gold.

Say aloud

RAW	LAW	SAW
SAD	BAD	DAD
FIRE	WIRE	LIAR

Let's write

Rearrange these words to form sentences:

grass and bushes from his body /After three days /covered /remove the.

____

consuming raw flesh of animals/ After many years Abing Taki started/ in the forest itself.

____

under the house through /Abotani's knife fell /bamboo floor of his house /the wide gaps of.

Let's do

- Go home and asked you parents to tell some local folktale?

- Note down the folktale told by your parents.

- Make some picture according to the story.

Teacher's Pages   Unit-5

This Unit is about sensitizing children to wildlife and supernatural power in nature along with their significance in the tribal society. Spend time in talking about universe, its creation and wildlife. Ask children how we can preserve the wildlife? Introduce them with various measures taken by the government to preserve the wildlife  such as wildlife sanctuary. And you are requested to read more stories on animals to them.

Develop listening skills

Read the text in a loud and suitable expression. Now after the completion of reading and discussing of the folktale, play a game with children. Start with asking them to close their eyes. Then hear and identify the following sounds as you or some children make them –

Roar like a Tiger
Meow like a Cat
Growl like a Bear
Moo like a Cow
Bellow like a Mithun
Hee-haw like a Donkey
Baah like a Goat
Scream like a Monkey

Now ask them to open their eyes and ask them to Meow like a ___________.

Ask the children say which animal it is. Similarly add other sounds.

Develop pronunciation

Say aloud with children the rhyming words like –

RAW   LAW   SAW

CLIMATE   MATE   PRIVATE

BIRTH   EARTH WARD

KINGDOM   FREEDOM   WISDOM

Exposure to language

Let the sight words be the names of animals, insects and birds that the children have seen. These can be hung on the class room walls of the school.

Develop speaking skills

Encourage children for recitation of folksong and have a 'group recitation' between the class groups. Praise them and appreciate their efforts. You are requested not to force children who are not ready for speaking.

Read the folktale and let children tell what might have happened if Abotani did not to cover Abing Taki's body with grasses and bushes in the forest. Also, if after three days' grass and bushes covered from his body was not removed. Ask the children to make the list/ chart of cat family. Also Reading folktale aloud, Repeated reading, Choral reading, storytelling and re-writing activities can be encouraged.

Develop writing skills

You can now expect children to look, imagine and write a few sentences on questions from the text, but remember to keep a check tag and see whether the children are able to hold the pencil with a firm grip, and ensure they are able to enjoy writing.

A class chart where everyone comes and writes their names of their favorite fruits and animals under their group (Red, Yellow, Blue, Green) is a wonderful opportunity to see them enjoy writing time.

To make the meaning clear to children encourage them to construct meaningful sentences of opposites from the folksong and folktale.

Getting ready to follow instructions

Teach the children never to break the promises they make and never to make one if they can't keep it. Make a group amongst the children and give them a trust game to play and instruct them.

Take the children to visit a zoo if possible and talk about not hurting or teasing the animals. Lastly, make a class collage and you are requested to assist them in every way possible from arranging the materials to completion of collage.